AF593716

Hoffnung IN HARMONY

SOUVENIR PRESS

First published 1985 by Souvenir Press Ltd,
43 Great Russell Street, London WC1B 3PA
and simultaneously in Canada

ISBN 0 285 62714 7

Printed and bound in Great Britain by William Clowes Limited,
Beccles and London

Introduction

Gerard Hoffnung had his first cartoons published at the age of fifteen, in the magazine *Lilliput.* Until his early death less than twenty years later, his output and versatility were prodigious: musical cartoons, drawings, illustrations, regular broadcasts on radio, appearances on television and the famous Hoffnung concerts of symphonic caricature, still enjoyed by audiences all over the world.

His art was that of a gentle man, always laughing with those he caricatured, never at them. Passionately fond of music, he loved to satirise its every aspect. The drawings in this book were made during the last two years of his life and bear his trademarks of keen observation, underlying kindness and lack of malice. Perhaps these are the reasons why his books continue to delight countless people throughout the world even now, more than twenty-five years after his death.

For a decade and a half after the Second World War, the Chelsea Arts School's New Year Ball was the highlight of the carnival season. Held at the Royal Albert Hall, it was patronised by almost every artist in London, both budding and arrived.

In 1957 Hoffnung was asked to design the decorations for the event and the following rough sketches, transformed into models, made the occasion one of the most successful in the history of the Chelsea Arts Ball.

Glass Ball over head
if possible
CH

This Accord
one side

ost sketch from
e Albert Hall to the other.

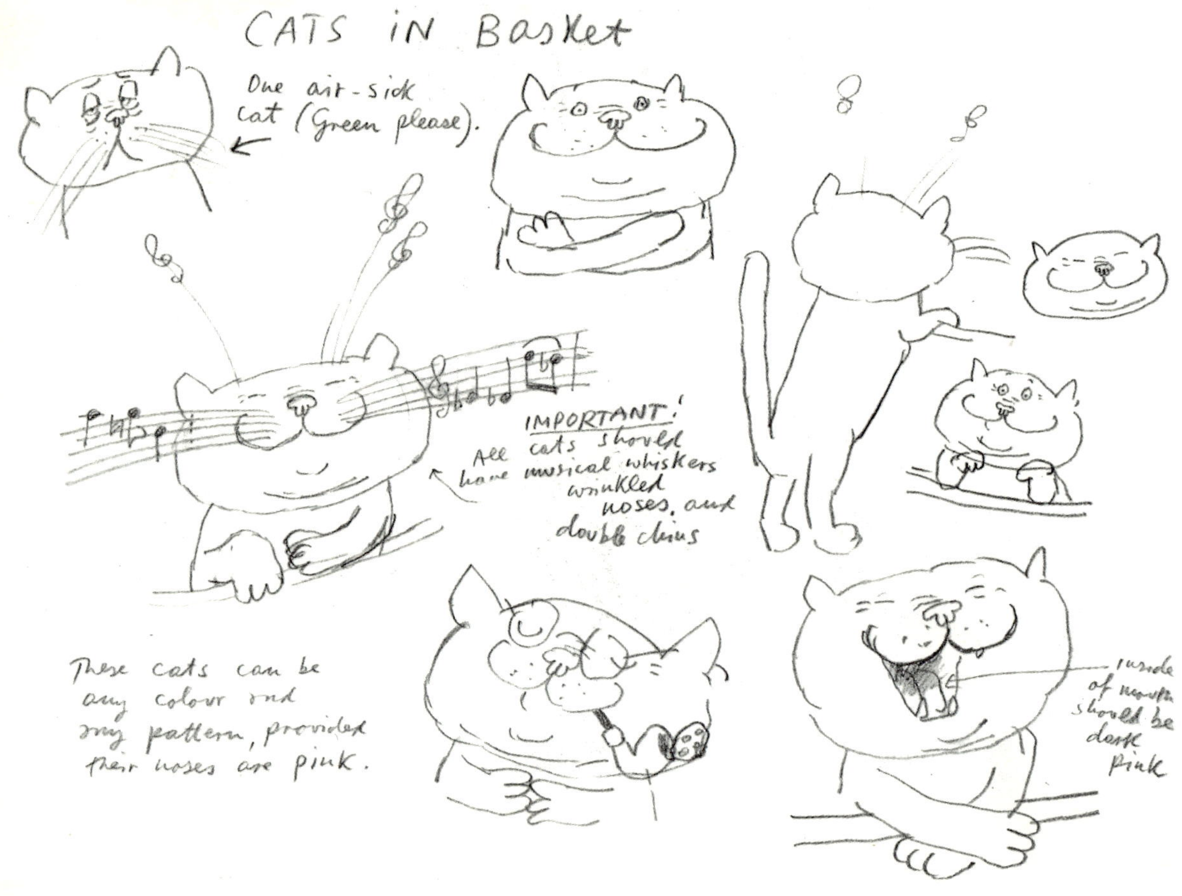

CATS IN BASKET
One air-sick cat (Green please).
IMPORTANT! All cats should have musical whiskers wrinkled noses, and double chins
These cats can be any colour and any pattern, provided their noses are pink.
Inside of mouth should be dark pink

These two Trombones must be <u>joined</u> thus and must stretch from one side of the hall to the other

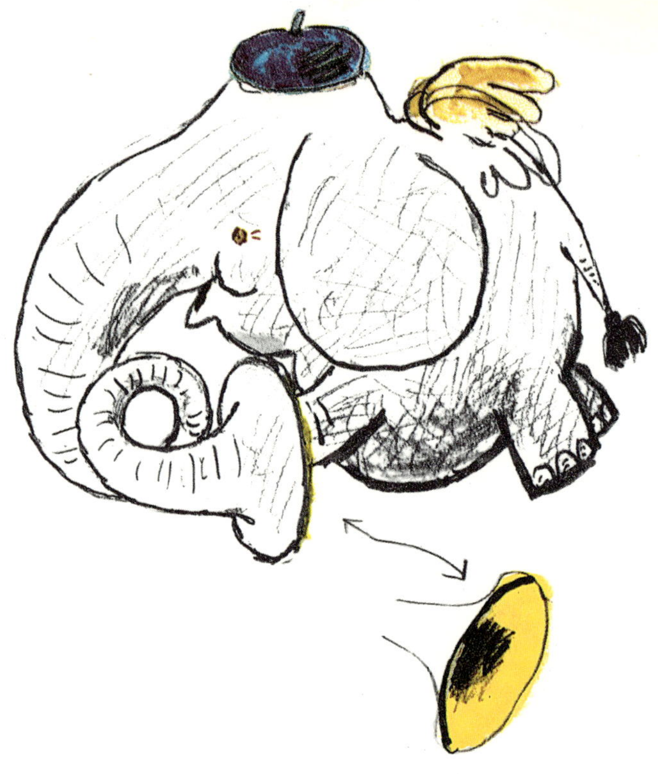

Chelsea Arts Ball

Notice on the
Back of one
of the Elephants
PLEASE
KNOCK,
Bell
OUT
OF
ORDER

This second
twist is
not
ccessary.
Can be
straight forward
like this

I would like to see
these Elephants flying
about in the air, or is
that impractible?

Glass Bell

This smoke need not be real, though I would prefer the latter personally, but cotton wool will do.

other side of Tuba

Chelsea Arts Ball

1958

HAROLD HOLT UNLIMITED IN ASSOCIATION WITH
THE LONDON COUNTY COUNCIL
PRESENTS:
The
Hoffnung
INTERPLANETARY
MUSIC FESTIVAL
1958
ROYAL FESTIVAL HALL
General manager: T.E. C.B.E.
FRIDAY 21st AND repeated
SATURDAY 22nd NOVEMBER
at 8. p.m.
HOFFNUNG SYMPHONY ORCHESTRA
CONDUCTOR: LAWRENCE LEONARD.
HOFFNUNG FESTIVAL OPERA COMPANY
AND CHORUS
THE BAND AND TRUMPETERS OF THE ROYAL MILITARY
SCHOOL OF MUSIK (Kneller Hall) by permission of the Commandant
Lieut. Col. David McBain. O.B.E.
THE DOLMETSCH ENSEMBLE.
THE MAESTRO (only appearance in this country)
MALCOLM ARNOLD
AARON COPLAND
CARL DOLMETSCH
NORMAN DEL MAR
AND A SURPRISE CAST OF HUNDREDS!
PRODUCER: COLIN GRAHAM.
An extravagant Gala Evening of Symphonic Caricature in glorious Hoffnungscope, with a repeat performance. Eleven World premières including THE UNITED NATIONS by Malcolm Arnold.
LET'S FAKE AN OPERA, an opera to end all operas by Reizenstein, and the first ever CONCERTO FOR CONDUCTOR AND ORCHESTRA by Francis Chagrin.
130 strong Symphony Orchestra loaded with Hoffnung surprises, together with many of the world's most distinguished composers and soloists. - Massed Bands and THE LOT !!!!!!
TICKETS ON SALE OCTOBER 21st
15/- 12/6 10/6 7/6 5/-
From: ROYAL FESTIVAL HALL BOX OFFICE (WAT 3191), CHAPPELL'S, 50 NEW BOND STREET (MAY 7600), USUAL Ticket Agents, and IBBS & TILLETT LTD., 124 WIGMORE STREET, LONDON W.1. (WEL 8418)
Postal applications for tickets should be accompanied by a stamped, addressed Envelope.
DRAWINGS REPRODUCED FROM THE HOFFNUNG CARTOON BOOKS BY PERMISSION OF DOBSON - PUTNAM.

The poster on the previous page announces the second of the two concerts of hilarious symphonic caricature produced by Hoffnung at the Royal Festival Hall in London during the 'fifties.

The dragon, Fafner, pictured below, pranced through the auditorium during a performance of 'Let's Fake an Opera'.

The Dragon, for:
"Let's fake an Opera"

Glyndebourne Opera, with its outsize programmes, rustic atmosphere and long sunny intervals, fired Gerard Hoffnung's imagination. The next three drawings are among those commissioned by the Glyndebourne Opera Company for one of their programmes

7. Wandering about the grounds, the visitor must be prepared for the unexpected.

One of the visiting artists relaxes.

This drawing was used one year by the Royal Festival Hall as a Christmas card.

The drawings on the front cover of this book, on the title page and in the following pages are among Hoffnung's last. The metal harp frame, originally incorporating a mirror, was bought in a Kensington antique shop and inspired the drawing it now contains.

Hoffnung